EVOLUTION & CULTURAL INFLUENCES OF MUSIC

LATIN

AND CARIBBEAN

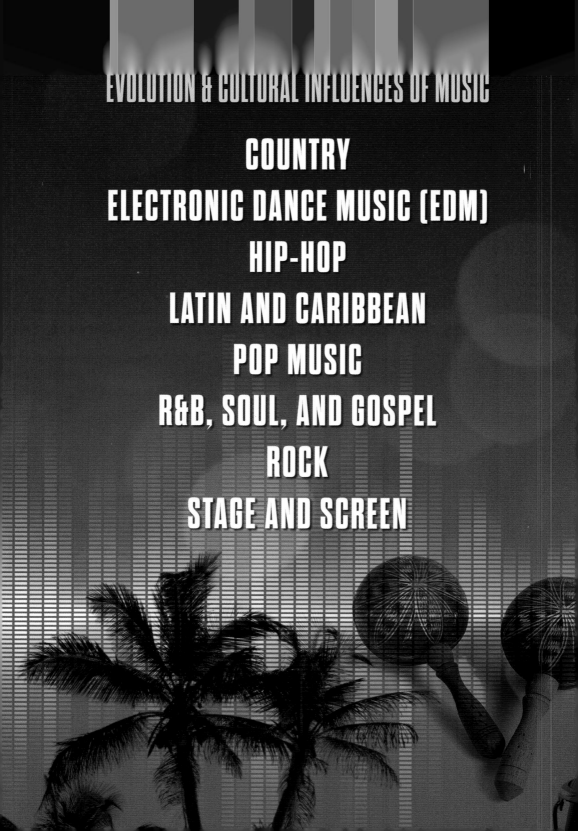

EVOLUTION & CULTURAL INFLUENCES OF MUSIC

COUNTRY

ELECTRONIC DANCE MUSIC (EDM)

HIP-HOP

LATIN AND CARIBBEAN

POP MUSIC

R&B, SOUL, AND GOSPEL

ROCK

STAGE AND SCREEN

EVOLUTION & CULTURAL INFLUENCES OF MUSIC

LATIN
AND CARIBBEAN

LARA STEWART MANETTA

MASON CREST
PHILADELPHIA | MIAMI

MASON CREST

450 Parkway Drive, Suite D, Broomall, Pennsylvania 19008
(866) MCP-BOOK (toll-free) • www.masoncrest.com

Printed and bound in the United States of America.

CPSIA Compliance Information: Batch #ECIM2019.
For further information, contact Mason Crest at 1-866-MCP-Book.

First printing

ISBN (hardback) 978-1-4222-4373-2
ISBN (series) 978-1-4222-4369-5
ISBN (ebook) 978-1-4222-7438-5

Library of Congress Cataloging-in-Publication Data on file at the Library of Congress.

Interior and cover design: Torque Advertising + Design
Production: Michelle Luke

QR CODES AND LINKS TO THIRD-PARTY CONTENT

CONTENTS

KEY ICONS TO LOOK FOR:

Words to Understand: These words with their easy-to-understand definitions will increase the reader's understanding of the text while building vocabulary skills.

Sidebars: This boxed material within the main text allows readers to build knowledge, gain insights, explore possibilities, and broaden their perspectives by weaving together additional information to provide realistic and holistic perspectives.

Educational Videos: Readers can view videos by scanning our QR codes, providing them with additional educational content to supplement the text. Examples include news coverage, moments in history, speeches, iconic sports moments, and much more!

Text-Dependent Questions: These questions send the reader back to the text for more careful attention to the evidence presented there.

Research Projects: Readers are pointed toward areas of further inquiry connected to each chapter. Suggestions are provided for projects that encourage deeper research and analysis.

Series Glossary of Key Terms: This back-of-the-book glossary contains terminology used throughout this series. Words found here increase the reader's ability to read and comprehend higher-level books and articles in this field.

Puerto Rican singer Luis Fonsi had a major hit in 2017 with his song "Despacito," which featured another Puerto Rican performer, the rapper Daddy Yankee. Music from Latin America and the Caribbean is growing more popular in the United States.

 # WORDS TO UNDERSTAND

polyrhythm—a rhythm that makes use of two or more different rhythms simultaneously.

syncopated—possessing an unexpected off-beat.

CHAPTER 1

The Roots of Latin and Caribbean Music

Caribbean music can be thought of as a rich and spicy stew where everything comes together and flavors everything else. At the root is the rhythms and traditions of Africa. Slaves brought to Caribbean islands preserved their culture in the only way they could: through remembered music, dance, and ceremony. In island countries like Cuba, Haiti, Jamaica, and others, this music was augmented by folk from Spain, classical music from France, and the forgotten yet still evident influence of the lost native cultures of the Taino and others.

Caribbean and Latin music has an outsized influence all over the world. In 2017, the Latin song "Despacito" spent more weeks on *Billboard* magazine's Hot 100 chart than any other song, in any language. More and more Latin hits cross over into the mainstream every year. This is, on some level, only fair—the elements and influences of Latin and Caribbean music come from all over the world. On another level, the growing popularity of Caribbean and Latin music can be seen as a triumph of dislocated, enslaved, and oppressed populations. The peoples of the Caribbean islands absorbed many influences and created an important genre of music all their own.

Indigenous Music in the Caribbean

As in many other parts of the Americas, the Caribbean already had indigenous peoples living there when explorers and colonists arrived from Europe. The largest Native American population was the Arawak (also called Taino). They lived on the island that Europeans named Hispaniola, which includes Haiti and the Dominican Republic, as well as on other nearby islands. Another major indigenous group was the Carib tribe, which lived on Puerto Rico and often fought with the Taino.

Indigenous Caribbean music was used in ceremonies and religious celebrations. In great ceremonies called *areito*, as many as 1,000 participants would dance and sing around the musicians. Common instruments included flutes, rattles, gourd scrapers, and slit drums. The music took the form of energetic chants with a call-and-response structure.

Eventually, however, the native populations were overrun by the invaders from Europe. Christopher Columbus and other Spanish explorers of the early sixteenth century unwittingly carried diseases that the Native Americans had no natural resistance to, such as smallpox. These killed many natives. In addition, wars between the Spanish and the natives, and attempts by the Spanish to enslave the Arawak and Carib peoples, all but eliminated the indigenous people of the Caribbean islands by the year 1600.

Today, just a few descendants of the Arawak people remain in small villages on the island of Dominica. The Arawak language, and other indigenous Caribbean languages, are largely extinct. Although the native populations did not survive contact, their music nonetheless had an impact on the music that eventually developed in the region.

Some of the instruments that were common among indigenous Caribbean natives are still used in music from the region today. Maracas are a type of rattle made from dried

Arawak natives witness Christopher Columbus's arrival on the island of San Salvador, October 12, 1492. Columbus's discoveries would inspire a wave of European colonization and conquest in North and South America as well as the Caribbean islands.

gourds. The seeds inside make a sound when shaken. Although these were first used in religious contexts, they are now a common instrument in Caribbean music from throughout the region. In a Latin music band, the maracas are often played by the singer.

Güiros, also known as gourd scrapers, are another percussion instrument. They're made up of a hollow object like a gourd, which is scraped using a comb or stick. Notches cut along one side are used to make a sort of rhythmic rasping sound. This instrument is prominent in Puerto Rican, Cuban, and other

Güiros and maracas are traditional Arawak instruments. A güiro was usually made from a dried gourd. A stick was rubbed against the carved side to produce the sound. The Arawak made maracas with gourds or shells that were filled with dried seeds.

forms of Latin American and Caribbean music. It plays a key role in the rhythm section of genres like trova, son, and salsa. The instrument is played with a combination of long and short strokes. Like the maracas, the *güiro* is typically played by the singer.

Slit drums, which are also known as tone drums, use openings on the outside of the instrument to provide different sounds. The indigenous people's slit drums were called *mayohuacans*. They were made from hollowed logs with H-shaped openings cut into them. Today, a wide array of slit drums are used in Caribbean music. Some provide a strictly percussive sound for keeping a beat, while others add melody.

African Music

The next ingredient in the combination that would eventually emerge as Latin and Caribbean music is music from the African diaspora. As the Spanish killed off the natives of the islands, they brought slaves from Africa to work in their place. The Spanish needed large numbers of workers for plantations that grew sugar cane and other valuable crops. Between the early 1500s and the 1830s, around four to five million African slaves were brought to the Caribbean islands to work in Spanish, Dutch, French, or British colonies.

Black communities in the Caribbean have exerted a strong influence on music all over the world. The Caribbean is the birthplace of musical icons ranging from the Jamaican reggae star Bob Marley to the current hip-hop figures Nicki Minaj and Rihanna. The latest dance music is as likely to reflect the rhythms of reggae as modern electronica.

While earlier historians were likely to argue that enslaved black communities did not retain great degrees of their traditional African cultural roots, newer interpretations reveal rich cultural and musical backgrounds that persist today.

There are many specific characteristics in Latin and Caribbean music that can be traced to Africa. In religious music like that associated with Haitian Vodou and Cuban Santería, listeners can find many melodies and words that even exist in African songs today.

In secular music, the influence can be felt as well. In African villages, music was usually an act of community participation. While soloists and featured performers had their part, most music was the work of the whole community, where people would contribute by singing, clapping, dancing or playing instruments. This can be heard today in music like Cuban son, which is characterized by heavy rhythms, a call-and-response structure, and large musical groups.

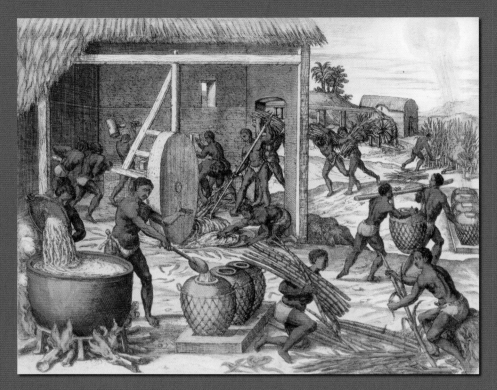

This illustration from 1595 shows African slaves processing sugarcane on a Caribbean plantation. Beginning in the 16th century, the Spanish imported millions of slaves from West Africa to work in Cuba and their other Caribbean colonies. Today, it is estimated that approximately 35 percent of Cubans are descended from African slaves.

African music had a massive emphasis on rhythm. It's no accident that some of the most notable Latin and Caribbean songs have been dance music. It's the product of the original African beats, which had a complexity that was novel against the measured meters of popular European music of the era. African music included complex rhythms called **polyrhythms**, where more than one beat would come together. They were also characterized by an interaction of regular beats and offbeat **syncopated** notes.

One African instrument that is commonly used is the *quijada*. It is literally made from the jawbone of a donkey, horse, or mule. The bone is stripped of tissue, then dried so that the teeth become loose. They rattle when the jaw is shaken, or when a stick is rubbed or tapped against it.

Musical Styles from Europe

Starting with Christopher Columbus's first trips to the Caribbean in the late fifteenth and early sixteenth century, Europeans began colonizing the islands. Their first goal was to find gold and silver. But not all places had an abundance of these precious metals. So the colonists had to find other ways to extract riches from the new lands. One way they did this was to begin producing and selling certain crops that could not be grown in Europe. Sugar was popular in Europe, but was expensive and hard to find. So the Spaniards established plantations to grow sugar cane, and shipped large quantities of sugar back to Europe. They also grew other crops for export, such as coffee, rice, and indigo.

The Dutch, British, French, and Spanish were all involved in the colonization of the Caribbean islands. However, the Spanish and French colonists probably had the strongest influence. They brought classical music from composers like Bach and Handel, along with folk songs and popular dance music. Many of these songs and musical forms had similar features to and a high level of compatibility with African music. For instance, many Spanish traditional songs used two and three part vocal harmonies, as did African music. The tradition of dancing in lines shows up in both European courts and African communities. European Christians celebrated seasonal festivals that live on as Caribbean *carnivals* today.

These forms all came together with other influences to create a modern music that is a unique combination. The degree of each place's influence will depend on the makeup of the population during their formative era. In a place like Puerto Rico where thousands of European settlers took root, the European influence was heavier. In a place like Haiti, where thousands of slaves would work under a handful of white overseers, a European influence was less pronounced. In the end, the music of each island and region has its own unique character.

Music from France and Spain

The French brought classical music and dances to the Caribbean through upper class forms like the waltz and minuet. The *quadrille*, a masked dance popular in the court of Napoleon, came to the French Caribbean islands in the early nineteenth century.

A European drew this picture of Afro-Caribbean slaves dancing in 1833. The slaves are accompanied by various percussion instruments, including drums and gourd rattles. Modern Caribbean music incorporates many traditional West African influences.

Scan here to see Dominican performers dancing a quadrille:

As in most of the Caribbean, slaves in places like Martinique were prohibited from playing drums or dancing to their native music. Like many restrictions on slaves' expression, the justification was down to fear: plantation owners feared secret communication in the drum beats and the unifying nature of the music itself.

However, the slave populations could not be subdued completely. As musicians charged with entertainment at plantation owners' parties, slaves learned to play the music of the French upper class. They developed a version of the quadrille dance all their own. Their version was a parody and burlesque, which they performed in their camps to mock the dominant class that enslaved them.

To this day, the local form of the quadrille continues to thrive. The dance and music form part of the background of *zouk*, a type of Caribbean music that became popular in the 1970s. This dance

Bongo drums were made from wood and covered with animal skins.

Conga drums are taller than bongos. They are used in Afro-Cuban music genres such as conga and rumba.

also remains an important symbol of Afro-Caribbean identity in a number of islands colonized by the French, British, and Dutch.

When the Spanish first began colonizing the areas that would someday become Puerto Rico and Cuba, they brought not only classical music but the region's popular dance and folk styles, as well.

The Spanish dance *bolero* was popular at the time Spanish colonization began. Its influence can be felt in *bachata*, a dance popular in the countryside of the Dominican Republic.

As mentioned before, some countries show more Spanish influence than others. Cuba and Puerto Rico are two places where heavy Spanish influence are still prominent today in language and musical styles. The two were once described as "two wings of the same bird" by Puerto Rican poet and journalist Lola Rodríguez de Tió because of the similarities of the culture and history. This is due, in part, to both places having been occupied by Spanish settlers for a long time. The musical influence can be felt today in the heavy ballads played on classical guitar.

European Instruments

Spanish guitar has been highly influential, both in its original form and in the *tres*, a six-stringed, three-chord adaptation invented in Cuba. There, it is the principal instrument in *son* music. The *tres* has been further modified in Puerto Rico, where the instrument has three chords and nine strings.

Woodwind instruments like the flute were necessary for the classical music that upper class European plantation owners played for their guests. These instruments were adapted to later Caribbean styles of popular music.

French colonists flee from rebellious slaves in the colony of Saint-Domingue, 1790s. When the Haitian revolt began, thousands of people, both black and white, left the island looking for safer places to settle. Some went to other islands, like Cuba, bringing with them French music and dance forms that would soon be integrated into Cuban culture.

The guitar emerged as a musical instrument during the Renaissance period in Europe. Guitars were very popular in Spain, and became identified with that country. As Spanish colonies were established throughout the Caribbean region, the guitar inevitably followed and became an important element of the music in these regions.

Botijos were originally made out of the jugs used to transport kerosene from Spain to Cuba. There, the bottles were cut on the top and the side. Water was added to create different notes. The lower the water level, the lower the note. Players would blow across the opening of the bottle to produce notes. This was often used for the base note in Cuban *son* music.

Coming Together

One of the other strong characteristics of populations in the Caribbean was their ability to take in other cultural traditions and synthesize something new. A Spanish guitar may be accompanied by an indigenous drum played at an African beat. Classical flute music may find itself played against a lively Caribbean rhythm. This process continued to develop over time. The result was wealth of unique sounds that were more than their individual parts.

TEXT-DEPENDENT QUESTIONS

1. What were three instruments that came from the indigenous peoples of the Caribbean?

2. What is the name of the dance slaves in the French-occupied islands adapted?

3. Which two Latin American countries have been called "two wings of the same bird?" Why?

RESEARCH PROJECT

Using the Internet or your school library, find out more about European settlers of a specific Caribbean country or territory. Find out when these colonists arrived, how long they stayed, and what musical influences they brought with them. In a two-page paper, discuss how the European music was adapted by Caribbean natives and what its influence is today.

Musicians with Latin American ties have been making a mark in the United States for decades. Shown here, at the 2016 American Music Awards, are the members of the pop group Fifth Harmony. From left to right: Dinah Jane Hansen, Lauren Jauregui, Normani Hamilton, Ally Brooke, and Camila Cabello. Jauregui is the daughter of Cuban immigrants, Brooke is of Mexican descent, and Cabello was born in Havana.

 WORDS TO UNDERSTAND

conservatory—a school where people study music.
contredanse—a formalized dance style where participants dance in rows facing one another.
creolization—the blending of cultures as seen in language, food and music.
emigrate—to leave one's country of birth to live in another country.
improvisation—the process of creating music on the fly without preparation.

CHAPTER 2

Growing Stronger

In the sixteenth and seventeenth centuries, a trip across the Atlantic to get from Africa or Europe to the Caribbean would take about six weeks in ideal conditions. If winds were unfavorable or weather was bad, the journey could take three months or more. Some ships would never arrive at their destinations at all. There was no communication between ships. People could go for months or years without word from home.

The distance from homelands wasn't the only factor that was changing how people in the Caribbean thought of themselves. In certain locales, island rule would pass from one group of conquerors to another, sometimes in periods of less than a year. Slave populations and European overlords would live in close proximity, passing bits of their inherited and newly developed cultures back and forth. Each had brought with them elements of their culture that they passed on to their children. Slaves were exposed to European culture by working in European households. In turn, those who worked within the households would share bits of their own music and history.

Social classes were rigid, but sometimes less rigid than history would have them appear. In some parts of the Caribbean, particularly Cuba, people of African descent gradually experienced a rise in social status, although they still often lived in segregation. Slaves in Cuba could, with money they earned in their off hours, buy their freedom. This was, incidentally, more common for women who were enslaved than it was for men. Female slaves were less expensive because of Cuba's high dependence on physical labor in the sugar cane fields. Additionally, the child of a slave owner and slave was free at birth. Freed slaves would often travel to the capital of Havana. They contributed to a thriving urban culture, including a colorful musical landscape.

In all areas of the Caribbean, a gradual change was occurring: people weren't thinking of themselves anymore as, say, Spaniards living on the island of Hispaniola or French citizens living in Jamaica. Instead, they were coming into an identity, and a group of cultures, all their own. They were becoming peoples of the Caribbean.

Creating a Caribbean/Latin Culture

The distance from their ancestral homelands and the gradual blending of both bloodlines and traditions eventually gave the Caribbean a culture that was something novel and decidedly modern.

When people from diverse backgrounds meet in a part of the world that is the homeland to neither, their languages will often combine. Each will discover nouns, verbs and turns of phrase from others' languages. Sometimes, they will learn a few words of each other's languages for practical interactions. Other times, they will pick up a phrase or two from a popular song.

The first generation of this blending is known as a "pidgin" language. When that language becomes the native tongue of their descendants, it becomes known as a creole. While creoles can be created in any part of the world, the term is most heavily associated with the blending of languages and cultures that occurred in the Americas.

During the 1950s, singer Harry Belafonte introduced the calypso music of Trinidad and Tobago to American audiences with hit songs like "The Banana Boat Song" and "Jump in the Line." The talented singer and actor from Jamaica would become one of America's most beloved entertainers, and was very active in the Civil Rights Movement of the 1950s and 1960s.

Creolization isn't a technical event—like adding two plus three to make five. Instead, there is that hard-to-quantify human element. People take the things that they like best from their own background and borrow what speaks to them from the other cultures that they encounter. They may be inspired by a melody and wonder what it will sound like on a different musical

African folk dancers perform on a street in Havana.

instrument. They may hear a word in a foreign language that expresses an idea that doesn't exist in their own. Or, they may be struck by the spirit of a fast-moving dance melody and decide to see what would happen when they apply that pace and beat to the folk songs they grew up with. The results become something that is not an obvious blend of two elements, but instead is sometime truly original and new.

The Caribbean was part of a New World. Caribbean people were conscious of their disparate histories, but also of the fact that they were no longer a part of the worlds that they came from.

Slaves forcibly taken from their home countries were forced to leave property and customs behind. French, Spanish, English and other settlers would have children in the new world who had never set foot in their parents' countries of origins. These people were not foreigners living far from their homes. They were something else altogether.

As Peter Manuel noted in his book *Caribbean Currents: Caribbean Music from Rumba to Reggae*:

> **The transition from being an African— or a European—to being a Caribbean is a key concept in the formation of Caribbean culture and music, embodied in the term** *"creolization,"* **which connotes the development of a distinctive new culture out of the prolonged encounter of two or more other cultures.**

The new culture and music was something modern that had never existed before. It had elements of the classical and folk music of European plantation owners. It also included both Indigenous and African influences. However, the more time went on, the more and more apparent it became that this part of the world had an infectious musical style all its own.

This new musical culture found expression in dozens or even hundreds of ways. Some were quickly widely accepted. Others were denounced by elites who had a more Eurocentric point of view. However, the styles there were rejected by those at the top still found a cultural foothold. Styles like calypso and son started off as something enjoyed by those considered lower class. Over time, these musical forms would become more and more sophisticated. Eventually, they would be accepted by the upper classes and widely considered essential Caribbean music.

There are dozens of examples of music working its way through Caribbean culture.

Cuban *Danzón*

The *danzón* is the national dance of Cuba. However, it was not always so widely loved and practiced. Once, it was considered highly scandalous and a dance not fit for civilized company. However, the initial resistance on the part of the elites of society would play out with new music again and again throughout Caribbean history.

The *danzón's* earliest roots can be traced, surprisingly, back to a European form of dancing known as **contredanse**. This highly stylized dance involving partners was very popular in the courts of England, Spain, and France. During the mid-seventeenth century, these countries vied for control of the islands and resources of the Caribbean.

The urban residents of Havana, Cuba, were roughly evenly

Tango music is usually played on guitars, or by an ensemble that includes violins, a flute, piano, double bass, and an accordion-like instrument called the bandóneyn.

divided between people who were white, black and those of mixed race. They adopted this very formal form of dance, with some changes. White residents were uncomfortable with the fluid movements in African dances, finding these motions scandalous. Black residents, by contrast, were just as likely to find male and female dancers touching while dancing uncouth. In African dances, men and women would dance together, but not make contact.

In the end, each took something they found daring from the other. Motions common to African dancing made their way into the new contredanse, which was performed with partners close together, but never touching.

Each contredanse began the same way: musicians would play a few bars of melody. During this time, dancers would chat, pick partners and get ready to get in formation. Then, after the introduction, they would dance in pairs in a series of practiced motions. The original English dance was performed to melodies played with European instruments like the fiddle, guitar, mandolin and flute. Havana musicians added new world percussion instruments like the guiro, which played lively African drum styles. They also slowed the tempo considerably.

The dance became wildly popular, especially with the lower classes of Cuba. Elites were scandalized, particularly when people of different races did these dances together. The danzón allowed them to interact freely in a way that their day to day lives did not yet permit.

Over time, the importance and value of this distinctive dance became understood and accepted. Today, the *danzón* is still performed throughout Cuba. Versions of the dance have found fans in Mexico. Puerto Rico also has its style. *Danzón* helped Cubans from different social classes and backgrounds appreciate one another, and so helped cement a more robust Cuban identity for everyone. It is danced each year during Carnival, and throughout the year at celebrations big and small.

Birth of the Tango

Cuba wasn't the only place that was developing musical styles and dances. In Argentina in the late nineteenth century, ranchers were becoming wealthy raising cattle and selling beef around the world. The most popular music in the capital city, Buenos Aires, was *milonga*. This music was especially popular in the poorer areas and among the indigenous and African diaspora populations.

A spirited dance done to accompany *milonga* music involved complex coordinated movements where partners would dance extremely close to one another, but never touch. Musicians would play songs heavy in **improvisation**. The music was played on Spanish instruments that included the guitar, violin, double bass, and a button accordion called the *bandoneon*.

Over time, the wealthy youth began to imitate and adopt the poor city dwellers' music and dancing. The dance became more sophisticated and the music more formal. Eventually, this dance and music would become a hit all over the world as the Tango, as movies and recording technology allowed music and dances to be shared more widely. While its popularity faded in other places over time, it remains one of the unique sounds and dances of Argentina.

Bolivia Embraces Its Culture

One common theme in the early development of Caribbean and Latin American culture was the elevation of European styles and denigration of the music and dancing of Indigenous and black Caribbean people. This was common even though, in most Caribbean and Latin American countries, there were more people of mixed heritage than not.

Some frictions eased on their own over time, through familiarity and shared culture. In other cases, a deliberate attempt was made to be more appreciative of all of the elements that made a particular region its own. Bolivia has thirty-four different

Scan here to watch a Bolivian group play a traditional song:

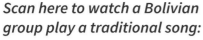

indigenous cultures. However, the majority belong to either the Aymara or the Quechua tribes. Taken together, these groups form the largest block of the rural population of Bolivia. They also make up a large part of the urban population, as well.

In the 1950s, the Bolivian government began encouraging more interest in and respect for the indigenous peoples in the region. The reason for this was to increase pride in local culture instead of elevating the music of Spanish occupiers. One of the results of this effort was a greater appreciation for the music they produced. The country created a folklore department in the Bolivian Ministry of Education. They sought to promote and capture the folk music of the Aymara and Quechua.

In 1965, Bolivian musician Edgar "Yayo" Jofré created a quartet he called Los Jairas in La Paz. Other area musicians followed suit. They created new sounds using indigenous instruments, like the zampoña pan flute and the lute-like stringed instruments such as the charango. However, the music still often retained Spanish influences, particularly when it was played in

Bolivia's urban centers. European instruments like guitar and violin became part of Bolivian folk's sound. Between the music of the colonists and that of the people who lived in the land before, they created a special new Bolivian folk sound that was unique.

Spicy Jamaican Sounds

Prior to the 1960s, the popular music in Jamaica was a form known as *men*to. This is lively, upbeat dance music very similar to calypso, and was not all that different from music that would be heard on other islands such as Barbados and the Virgin Islands.

However, the growing popularity of American rhythm and blues (R&B) resonated with Jamaican musicians. As American records became available on the island, they were played at parties known as sound systems. These parties were especially popular in areas where only a fraction of the population had access to electricity. While not everyone could listen to music at home, many were near enough to go listen at a party.

The innovative African-American musicians who would change their own country's sounds had a strong impact in this island country, as well. Musicians in Jamaica began recording covers of American R&B. These recordings were very loyal to the originals, but they were wildly popular with Jamaican audiences. To feed the desire for this music in Jamaican dancehalls, local groups began improvising and creating new songs of their own.

This music gradually started to sound less like American rhythm and blues and more like something else entirely. The new music, with influences from homegrown styles, was known as ska. Musicians slowed the beat and reincorporated the dance flourishes from mento and calypso.

The innovation only continued as Jamaican musicians found their stride. A form of music called rocksteady soon followed ska. The musicians in Jamaica who created rocksteady were well-versed in genres that included ska, as well as blues, jazz and traditional African drumming. Rocksteady used these elements

Jamaican singer Jimmy Cliff was an early star of ska music. He later became a groundbreaking reggae artist, helping that musical style gain international attention.

along with a slowed-down speed to make a new dance hall sound. Part of what made rocksteady so distinctive was its "one drop" beat, which placed emphasis on the third beat of every bar. In contrast to rock and roll, which typically puts the emphasis on the first beat (also called the "down beat"), this provided a more relaxed rhythm evocative of the tropics. Because of the influence of American popular music, rocksteady songs often had romantic themes. Rocksteady artists often covered the love songs popular on American radio.

Rocksteady would reach its highest popularity from 1966 to 1968. During this time, Jamaican youths were flooding from the countryside into urban areas. Many did not have strong confidence in the optimistic post-revolutionary climate. These youths became known as "rude boys" and they began to create a genre of music that fit the name.

Reggae was faster, more aggressive and more political than either ska or rocksteady. Where ska and rocksteady songs were traditional love songs, reggae pulled themes from the growing Rastafarian religion. The songs often had revolutionary themes, as well as religious and spiritual ones of universal love. Lyrics called on people, especially black and Caribbean people, to rebel against oppression. The first reggae record was a song called "Bangarang," which was released in 1968.

The music found fertile ground not just in Jamaica where it originated, but also in the United States, which was also undergoing strife and social change. In this way, Jamaican music sent waves out into the world that were equal to the ones shaping music back at home.

Cuba in Isolation

In some areas, part of developing a unique Caribbean identity was a product of a country becoming separated from outside influences. In the first half of the twentieth century, the influence of Cuban music continued to grow in the Caribbean and throughout the world. However, all of that changed when Fidel Castro took power in 1959.

An embargo on the part of the United States soon followed. The flow of Cuban records and musical styles was cut off abruptly. Very little Cuban music made it out of the country for decades after, and little music made it into the country, as well.

Under Castro, however, Cuba made culture, especially music, a priority. Counsels and schools were established to support musical education. Musicians who were educated in Cuba during that time speak often of extensive classical music education in conservatories, schools that focus on musical education. Musicians who now play styles that include salsa, rumba and jazz say that this classical education forms a very important part of their personal sound.

At the same time, the ideals of Cuba's revolution meant

MARIACHI MUSIC

One of the most famous forms of traditional music is mariachi, which originated in the string bands of rural Michoácan, Mexico. Originally, the mariachi bands' instruments included guitar, *vihuela* (a small five-string guitar), one or two violins, and a harp or guitarrón (a large bass guitar). In the 1930s, brass instruments like trumpets were added to the bands.

an opportunity for lower class Afro-Cubanos to integrate into mainstream Cuban society. People from that background, who had been barred from beaches, hotels, clubs, and restaurants during pre-Revolutionary times, were now allowed access.

Additionally, while the problems with state-owned media can't be overstated, they did provide one advantage that did not exist in the world outside of Cuba: musical expression free of commercial interest. There was none of the payola, soda or liquor brand sponsorship and other commercial factors that affected music in other parts of the Americas.

The result was a musical culture that continued to innovate and develop, albeit without an international audience. In the United States, in fact, many were told that the Cuban revolution had killed local music. This was far from the truth; Cuban music continued to develop even during the years of isolation.

A Culture of Innovation

If Caribbean music can be summed up in a word, that would be "innovation." When colonial overlords banned slaves from partaking in African drumming, music, songs or religion, that didn't lead to a wholesale adoption of European music, as hoped.

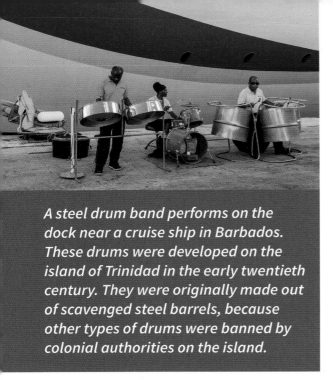

A steel drum band performs on the dock near a cruise ship in Barbados. These drums were developed on the island of Trinidad in the early twentieth century. They were originally made out of scavenged steel barrels, because other types of drums were banned by colonial authorities on the island.

Instead, it led to new sounds that fit into the place of the old and forbidden ones. In Trinidad, English plantation owners forbid the playing of African drums. They feared the sound and described it as savage. They also secretly suspected that the drums were used to transmit covert messages and to foment slave revolts.

The slaves, deprived of their beloved drums, soon found a replacement. They took metal barrels and banged them into new instruments. It was discovered that hammering the bottoms into concave shapes with different thicknesses produced different sounds. The steel drum was born. It quickly became a staple in the music of Trinidad, Jamaica and beyond.

As the digital age increases our access to one another's music and cultures, the thirst in Latin America and the Caribbean for new sounds has not been sated.

Today, musicians in the region continue to sample, mix and experiment from music from all over. Modern hip hop and R&B are just one well-known influence. However, tastes go even further afield.

Rhythms and melodies from African and Indian music have been incorporated for a musical mixture known as "chutney." The form, which incorporates Indian folk music played over the rhythms of *soca*, is popular carnival music in Trinidad. The digital era means that influences can be passed back and forth, with each side selecting an element and adding new musical spices to the mix.

TEXT-DEPENDENT QUESTIONS

1. Where did contredanse originate?
2. What is the national dance of Cuba?
3. What was the first reggae record?

RESEARCH PROJECT

The cultures that lived side by side in most Caribbean countries were often somewhat isolated from one another. However, each would gradually influence the other through culture and music. Describe a musical form that developed in the Caribbean and the influences that created it. Using quality online or offline resources, research one musical form and trace its historic origins. Describe the changing attitudes toward this musical form over time, as well as examples of this musical form that exist today.

A Cuban band performs son *music in Santa Clara City.* Son *combines the structure and feel of traditional Spanish songs with Afro-Cuban percussion and other influences. It is the basis for many popular types of Latin music, including mambo, timba, and salsa.*

 WORDS TO UNDERSTAND

diaspora—people who have left their homeland in great numbers.

populous—having a high population.

CHAPTER 3

Going Mainstream

The Caribbean and Latin American region has an influence that, given its relatively small geographic area and population size, completely outsized. During the region's formative years, they took influences from outside and made them all their own. Later on, as radio, records and trans-Atlantic flights became common, Latin America and the Caribbean would share their influences in return. The early twentieth century saw music from these areas going mainstream and giving the rest of the world a sound it had not heard before. The influence continues to this day.

Time to Tango

Uruguay's and Argentina's lively dance found its way into mainstream Western consciousness through a circuitous route. The music and dance made it to the United States by way of Paris, and through the stages of Broadway.

By the early 1900s, the dance had become extremely popular in both countries. It may have stayed a regional favorite, however, had an Argentinian band not traveled to Paris to record tango music sometime around 1910. The music was an instant hit among Paris's high society. By 1913, all of Europe was in the grip of tango fever.

That same year, a famous British dancing team, husband

Dancers perform the distinctive tango that was created in the nineteenth century to accompany Argentine and Uruguayan tango music.

and wife duo Irene and Vernon Castle, found themselves stranded in Paris after losing their jobs mid-tour. They made a comeback by learning the tango and were a huge sensation with audiences.

The next year, they took their act across the Atlantic and began performing the tango on Broadway. Audiences were enamored of the sensuous dance and were eager to learn it themselves.

The tango represents the first dance that unseated European styles in favor of the contributions from the Americas. The Castles opened the first Castle School of Dancing and classes were immediately in demand. Castle Tango Palaces opened up throughout the US, bringing this exciting new dance form to every major city.

World War I led to a brief interruption in the tango craze. In Europe, where the dance had continued to thrive, fighting across the continent sent Argentinian musicians back home. Nightlife in the United States cooled as America joined the war effort.

However, when the conflict was over, the tango was waiting. In the post-War era, tango fever burned hotter than ever before. Then-unknown Italian actor Rudolph Valentino performed a tango with actress Beatrice Dominguez in the silent movie *The Four Horsemen of the Apocalypse* (1921). This is considered the first filmed version of the tango. The movie was a hit and the tango became more popular than ever.

Singer Carlos Gardel was born in France but moved to Argentina with his mother when he was just two years old. He learned folk and tango music there and began to tour as a professional singer. His timing was perfect. In the mid-1920s, he was touring and performing right as the world fell in love with the tango. He would go on to perform tango music in a number of influential movies that included *Tango Bar* and T*ango on Broadway*. In all, Carlos Gardell would record roughly 900 tango songs. Gardel died in 1935 in a plane crash and the tango craze faded soon after, to be replaced with other popular dances and music from the Americas. However, the tango retains appeal and is still performed both recreationally and competitively in places throughout the world.

CULTURAL ACHIEVEMENT

On August 31, 2009, the tango was added to the Intangible Cultural Heritage list maintained by the United Nations Educational, Scientific, and Cultural Organization (UNESCO) after a joint proposal from Argentina and Uruguay. "The music, dance and poetry of tango both embodies and encourages diversity and cultural dialogue," noted UNESCO. "It is practiced in the traditional dance halls of Buenos Aires and Montevideo, spreading the spirit of its community across the globe even as it adapts to new environments and changing times."

Cuba Rumbles with Rumba and Son

Cuba is the largest island in the Caribbean and also its most **populous**. Located just 90 miles south of Key West, Florida, Cuba is also our closest Caribbean neighbor. Cuba, formerly a colony of Spain, threw off Spanish rule in the 1898 and became a republic in 1902. This led to a closer relationship with the United States, with an exchange of technology and culture. Between all of these factors, it was inevitable that Cuba's music would go mainstream in the States.

In the earliest parts of the modern age, music did not spread as quickly and fluidly as it does today. Before the modern era, the only way to hear new music was to travel to a new place or to see a touring band perform. Records changed that, by bringing recorded music to the masses. However, not everyone could afford record players, or the power to use them.

Radio made new music more accessible than ever. Cuba was the first place in the Americas to have radio broadcasts, and they aided the spread of Cuban music considerably. The first commercial radio station began broadcasting on October 10, 1922. Its transmission was broadcast across Cuba and the rebroadcast in a club in Key West. This broadcast consisted of a speech from the president of Cuba, followed by the playing of classical and Cuban music.

Cuban music, including *son* and rumba took audiences by storm. Rumba first developed in Cuba in the nineteenth century. Its influences included both religious *Santería* drumming and the call-and-response form that was growing in popularity in secular music. In a call-and-response song, a singer will call out a line or a verse. Back-up singers will call back a chorus. Rumba will typically feature one or two dancers, as well. The music ensemble typically includes percussion instruments like conga drums and claves, sticks that are tapped together for a sharp sound.

The highly popular *danzon* music saw innovation in the 1920s, when it morphed into the street music known as son.

The famed Trío Matamoros is fondly remembered by Cubans today. This Cuban postage stamp artwork depicts Miguel Matamoros, Rafael Cueto, and Siro Rodríguez.

Son featured a rich mix of Spanish and Afro-Cubano influences. Bands like Sexteto Habanero recorded *son* music, which was distributed throughout the Caribbean and the United States.

The biggest *son* song to hit the United States was the song "El Manicero," which translates as "The Peanut Vendor." The words are simple: just a series of simple verses asking the listener whether they would like to buy a bag of delicious peanuts. However, the slow and moving delivery captured listeners' affection. The song's popularity was boosted when Will Rogers mentioned it in one of his columns. By 1931, the tune was a national hit and would stay on the charts throughout the summer of that year.

Band leaders in the United States were initially stumped when it came down to how to make this music danceable.

Cuban orchestras such as this one were very popular entertainment in the United States during the 1930s and 1940s. Their rhumba music was basically a blend of Cuban son and American big-band-style jazz.

However, they soon hit on the solution of simplifying and speeding up the time, which extended the song's reach into dance clubs throughout the nation.

Perhaps the most dramatic development in *son* music came at the hands of band leader Arsenio Rodriguez. Rodriguez was an Afro-Cubano tres player who also composed and arranged son music. He was blind, having been permanently injured as a child after being kicked by a horse. As a band leader, he made larger son ensembles popular. Typically, he would play with a conga, piano, and two or three trumpet players in his band. The result was music that had the carefree spirit of traditional street *son*, with a tighter, more traditional dance music feel. In the early 1950s, Rodriguez moved to New York city. There, his unique sound laid the foundations for salsa music. Due to poor health and economic problems, Rodriguez would not get the chance to personally benefit from this musical revolution. However, by the end of his life, salsa would become one of the dominant music forms in the Latin American music scene.

Mambo Madness

The mambo was the next big music craze to make it into the mainstream both within Latin America and up into the United States. In the 1940s, band leader Perez Prado popularized mambo in Havana. Prado had traveled back and forth between Cuba and the United States, where he heard American jazz. He incorporated this music into Cuban son.

Prado worked frequently with the singer Benny Moré, who had been born a slave in Southern Cuba. Moré moved to Havana when he was young and made a living singing son in the streets. He was discovered there by a record producer in 1948, who introduced him to Perez Prado and his band. Together, they went to New York to perform in famous clubs like the Stork Club.

In the first half of the 1950s, this music continued to grow in America, where it was among the most popular played in dance halls, particularly in Los Angeles. Mambo had its roots in son and rumba, but also owed much of its sound to emerging Latin Jazz. Mambo featured faster rhythms and even bigger bands that expanded on the theme that Arsenio Rodriguez had begun.

Mambo, in turn, helped drive the developing sound of salsa. While salsa's original architect was not able to benefit from his creation, other creators like Cuban band leader Machito and vocalist Celia Cruz, were there at the right time to see salsa's rise.

Salsa's Swing

While Latin music spread widely up until the late 1950s, the 1960s were a less auspicious time for that music genre. Rock and roll

Innovative Dominican bandleader and musician Johnny Pacheco coined the term "salsa" to describe the emerging Latin music of the 1960s and 1970s. He received a Latin Grammy Lifetime Achievement Award in 2005.

was taking the place of the big jazz bands. The big Latin ballrooms did not attract the same crowds that they once did.

Record labels that churned out Latin dance records were not actively promoting them. Only two small labels continued to put any energy into this niche.

Finally, the embargo against Cuba meant that Cuban music was no longer getting off the island and up to the United States. However, while this was happening, the Puerto Rican **diaspora** who had congregated in the New York area continued to crave sounds that reflected their island heritage more than the Anglo-centric music that was often heard on the radio.

These people began to look at rumba, *son* and mambo not as specifically Cuban music, but instead as pan-Latin creations. They expanded their influences and looked at all of the music that was being made in Latin American countries and worked to continue its development.

Dominican band leader Johnny Pacheco began showcasing salsa music through his small record label, Fania Records. At first, he sold records to stores in the New York area from the trunk of his car. However, soon, he found backers who allowed him to scout out new talent and develop new Latin sounds.

"In my opinion, the true salsa sound of that era was the musical fusion of New York with Puerto Rico, with Cuba and with Africa," said one modern salsa artist, Sergio George. "That whole fusion was for me the true roots of salsa in the late '60s and early '70s. It came out of a street sound, a barrio sound. People jamming in the park and someone coming to sing…. That was the raw street salsa sound."

Fania coined the term *salsa* for the music. Salsa, which means "hot sauce," was a frequent exclamation from the podium when bandleaders were leading a particularly energetic band. It was also the name of a popular Venezuelan radio show.

While many musicians consider salsa simply a commercial term for *son* and rumba music, others say that salsa added new innovations. Puerto Rican musical elements, such as new singing styles, became popular. Bands added non-traditional instruments, such as trombones and timbales. Jazz style solos became a common fixture in salsa songs.

Salsa songs also tackled new topics. There were, and are, many salsa songs that deal with traditional themes like romantic love. However, salsa was also more likely to contain political themes, such as pan-Latin solidarity and pride.

Politics and Protest

The new Latin Americans were not the only ones seeing upheaval. In the 1950s through 1970s, protest songs lit Latin and Caribbean airwaves on fire. Countries throughout the region were throwing off the binds of their colonial leaders. In some cases, unfortunately, the revolutionary leaders became dictators as soon as they took office. Individual musicians would create music to rouse supporters to create a national identity of their own. And, then, they would find that they were fighting against the governments that they had helped raise to power.

This revolutionary zeal was reflected in actions outside the Caribbean, as well. The American Civil Rights movement sparked an interest in music made by people of color not just in the United States, but in neighboring countries, as well. Participants in the Vietnam-era antiwar movement were looking for music with meatier themes than the love songs common in early rock and roll.

The Harder They Come

One of the styles of music that found eager audiences outside of its native area was reggae. The themes of resistance, solidarity and universal love were extremely popular with audiences in the US, Britain and other parts of the globe.

Although reggae had been growing in popularity in its native Jamaica since 1968, it wasn't until the early 1970s that audiences

Claves are a percussion instrument typically made from rosewood. They are played by being struck together.

outside of the island got a chance to hear this new and distinctive sound. The Jamaican crime film *The Harder They Come* was a surprise hit with a lively reggae soundtrack. The movie was filmed in Jamaica, where audiences loved seeing its naturalistic portrayal of Jamaican people and life. New Line Cinemas picked up the film in 1973 to distribute it in the United States. While it did not make a strong impression in its first run, it gained cult classic status when it was played as part of midnight movie showings.

The movie's soundtrack, however, was an even bigger hit. It featured a number of reggae songs from artists who included Jimmy Cliff, DJ Scotty, The Melodians, Desmond Dekker, the Slickers, and Toots and the Maytals. The soundtrack sold well in both the United States and in the UK and climbed to #140 on the *Billboard* chart of the 200 top albums.

This record opened up the way for many reggae artists to gain popularity in the United States. Bob Marley and the Wailers, for instance, were beloved for their crisp sound and inspirational lyrics. Throughout the 1970s the group would perform around the world to eager audiences.

A memorial in Jamaica to guitarist Peter Tosh. The reggae pioneer was one of the original members of the Wailers, along with Bob Marley and Bunny Wailer. The Wailers were the foremost reggae band of the 1960s and 1970s. Both Tosh and Wailer left the group in the mid-1970s and found success as solo reggae performers.

Latin American Contributions to Rock and Roll

As rock and roll emerged in the United States during the late 1950s, one Mexican-American star in particular gained special prominence. Ritchie Valens, born in California to Mexican parents, had a brief but pivotal role in the developing sound of rock and roll. He had several hits, including "Donna," which reached #2 on the *Billboard* charts. However, the hit song he is most known for is "La Bamba," which remains a well-known classic.

Valens did not write "La Bamba." The song was a popular Mexican folk song that was commonly played at weddings in the Veracruz region of Mexico. It was released as the B-side to "Donna," but soon became a hit in its own right. When *Rolling Stone* magazine ranked the "500 Greatest Songs of All Time" in 2004, Valens's version of "La Bamba" was the only non-English language song on the list.

"La Bamba" has been covered by many artists over the years, with each adding their own Latin touches. Mexican-American singer Trini Lopez included a live version on his debut album in 1963. "La Bamba" would return to the *Billboard* charts again in 1987, when the Latin-influenced Los Angeles rock band Los Lobos recorded a version for a Ritchie Valens **biopic**. Their version reached #1 on the charts in both the United States and the United Kingdom.

Mariachi musicians play a lively folk version of La Bamba:

Mainstream and Underground

Not all of the music that is inspired by Latin American or Caribbean sounds is heard in the American mainstream. Some is found in underground genres. Ska, for instance, lives on to this day as a subgenre of punk music. Its influence can be heard today in the sounds of American groups like Goldfinger and Reel Big Fish. The reggaetón variant had a huge underground following for years before breaking out on American radio.

TEXT-DEPENDENT QUESTIONS

1. What movie popularized reggae outside of Jamaica?
2. Which film was most instrumental in popularizing the tango?
3. Name three factors that contributed to the fall in popularity of Latin music in the 1960s.

RESEARCH PROJECT

Throughout the twentieth century, music from Latin America and the Caribbean found popularity with audiences in the United States, Britain, and throughout Europe. Using trusted online sources and your school library, research one artist who brought Caribbean and Latin American music to popularity in other parts of the world. Explore their early life and the lasting influences of their music, worldwide.

Christina Aguilera poses with her star on the Hollywood Walk of Fame in 2010. She helped to launch the popularity of "Latin pop" in 1999.

 WORDS TO UNDERSTAND

phonetically—repeating an unfamiliar (often foreign) word based on the sounds, without knowing the word's meaning in its native language.

propagate—to spread.

standards— musical compositions with established popularity, considered part of the "standard repertoire" of one or more musical genres. These pieces often serve as a base for musical improvisation.

CHAPTER 4

Taking Hold Around the World

Latin American and Caribbean musicians weren't just wowing audiences through the 1940s and 1950s. They were also inspiring the musicians who heard them play. Jazz and big band musicians recognized something truly groundbreaking and different in the Latin sound. They, in turn, took a page from their Caribbean neighbors and began to include these influences in music of their own.

"Manteca" Becomes a Jazz Standard

On September 29, 1947, Dizzy Gillespie performed at Carnegie Hall. This is, understandably, a high point in any musician's career. However, the performance was a pivotal one not just for Gillespie, but also for the course of American jazz as a whole. Attendees expected that they were about to hear a showcase of bebop jazz from one of the architects of this genre. What they were treated to instead was one of the first inclusion of Latin rhythms into jazz.

Just a few days before the performance, Gillespie had been introduced to Chano Pozo, a Cuban conga player. Pozo was young, athletic-looking, and eager to share his music in the United States. The two decided right away that they would team up to create a Latin big band. One of the first songs they

Percussionist Chano Pozo played an important part in the development of Latin jazz. He was a major influence on jazz legend Dizzy Gillespie.

played together for the Carnegie Hall audience was "Manteca." This song replaced more conventional drum sections with driving Afro-Cuban conga drums. The horn section played an aggressive polyrhythmic beat. During the performance, Pozo strode around the stage chanting in Yoruba, an African language that enslaved people had brought to Cuba in previous centuries. The language had been preserved in popular Cuban customs, as well as in Caribbean religious practices like Santería.

The inclusion of Afro-Cuban jazz in the performance made Latin Jazz a US sensation overnight. In later interviews, Gillespie characterized the reaction as "similar to a nuclear weapon." In December of that year, Gillespie took to the studio to record his new sound. The record was the first to include the clave in a jazz record. Gillespie said, "they'd never seen a marriage of Cuban music and American music like this before." Contemporaries characterized Dizzy Gillespie as an intellectual who was deeply curious about other cultures. He had a deep interest in African cultural influence and was eager to include it and Cuban sounds in his music.

Chano Pozo was born in Havana in 1915 and emigrated to New York in 1946, where he met Cuban trumpet player Mario Bauzá. Pozo's two top instruments were the bongo and conga drums, but he was also a gifted composer and dancer. While he was instrumental in bringing Latin Jazz to life, he sadly did not get to enjoy his accomplishment long. In 1948, he was shot and killed in a Harlem bar. However, his impact, along with Gillespie's, lives on to this day.

Gillespie was instrumental in maturing the sound of Latin Jazz. Jazz influences had been a big part of Cuban dance music for some time. But, Gillespie's new band was the first to present Latin-infused jazz as music meant for thoughtful listening, instead of a soundtrack and backdrop for dancing. Songs like "Manteca" and "Tin Tin Deo," which were cowritten by his collaborator Chano Pozo, became influential **standards**.

Scan here to see Dizzy Gillespie's jazz band perform "Manteca":

Tito Puente appears at the 2000 Grammy Awards ceremony with an award he received for best Tropical Latin Album. Puente's influential career lasted for more than fifty years.

The strong push and pull rhythms that characterize those songs can also be heard in subsequent music. Top examples include Bobby Parker's hit "Watch Your Step," the Beatles's "I Feel Fine," and "Tequila," performed by Mexican-American group The Champs in 1958.

The King of Latin Music

Tito Puente was born in Manhattan in the Harlem Hospital Center. He was the son of Puerto Rican immigrants. As a hyperactive child living in a cramped apartment, he often caused neighbors to complain when he'd spend hours banging on pots and pans. His mother sent him for piano lessons at a cost of 25 cents a week. By the time he was ten, he had switched from piano to drums. He became familiar with local club owners when started a dance act with his sister at the age of thirteen. When Latin jazz bandleader Machito's drummer was drafted into the army at the beginning of World War II, Tito Puente took his place, becoming a professional musician.

Puente was drafted himself in 1942 and spent three years in the US Navy. He returned to New York in 1945 and used his money from the G.I. Bill to study music at the famed Juilliard School. After graduation, he formed a band that would eventually be known as the Tito Puente Orchestra.

It was the right time for this innovative Latin music. His band played mambo in dance clubs throughout New York, making him a Latin music sensation. His popularity reached the Caribbean, as well. In 1952, he was the only non-Cuban invited by the Cuban government to participate in a government-sponsored "50 Years of Cuban Music" event.

In 1958, he released his best-selling album *Dance Mania*. More records followed, each bringing different aspects of Latin sound to American audiences.

Fans connected with the way that Puente would put a polished and studied jazz shine on traditional Latin dance music, as well as his enthusiastic performances. In an era when many Latin artists incorporated political themes or social criticism in their work, Puente was resolutely cheerful and dance-oriented. "What else have I got to sell?" he said when he was once asked about his ebullient style. "I'm not Ricky Martin, to wave my hips

THE IMPORTANCE OF TITO

In 2002, Tito Puente's 1958 album *Dance Mania* was added to the National Recording Registry, an official list of albums that are culturally or artistically significant in the history of the United States. It is also included in Universe Publishing's *1001 Albums You Must Hear Before You Die.* Thanks to his influence, Tito Puente was nicknamed "El Rey"—the King.

around and show my belly button. I don't have a girl in front of the band singing. I need the people to see I'm having a good time."

His music included takes on Afro-Cuban and Latin dances that included the mambo, merengue, cha-cha, bossa nova, and salsa. Throughout his career, he played with leading jazz performers and symphony orchestras alike. He was a tireless touring artist, often playing hundreds of times in a year. His work brought him many awards, including five Grammys. His most famous song, "Oye Como Va," became well-known to modern audiences after being covered by Carlos Santana's rock group.

Rumba Across the Ocean

In the middle of the twentieth century, rumba wasn't just making waves in the West. International trade led to Latin and Caribbean music finding a thriving home in the Congolese Basin of Africa.

Starting in the 1930s, record companies sought to increase their profits by repackaging Cuban recordings and selling them to new audiences in Ghana, Nigeria, and the Congo region of Africa. These included recordings by popular Cuban son groups like Septeto Habanero, Trío Matamoros, and Los Guaracheros de

Oriente. The records were frequently played by Radio Congo Belge, a radio station with a powerful transmitter that reached audiences in many areas. Local musicians began adding these new sounds to their repertoires. The sound of Cuban son was both familiar and welcome to African audiences. Because of the roots of son in the music preserved and **propagated** by African slaves brought to the new world, the resemblance is unsurprising.

Bands that added the sounds of son to their music were known as "soukous," taken from a word that means "to shake." At first, the musicians would do straight covers of Cuban songs, singing the Spanish language lyrics **phonetically**. Later on, they would begin writing original creations in French and local languages. The parts of son music traditionally played by Cuban brass instruments would, instead, be adapted to be played on guitar.

Rumba is a type of percussion music that originated in northern Cuba. Dancing and singing are important elements of the music.

Puerto Rican singer Ricky Martin started his career in the late 1980s as a member of the teen singing group Menudo. In the 1990s he became a solo artist and scored big hits with salsa-influenced pop, including "Livin' la Vida Loca."

The resulting music was known as African rumba, even though it was more deeply based on son. Antoine Kolosoy, also known as Papa Wendo, became African rumba's first star, and toured Europe and North America in the 1940s and 1950s. Just as big bands became more and more popular in the West, they also gained a following in Africa. These bands would often fuse Cuban music with African folk for a new sound.

The music stayed popular all the way through the 1970s. After experiencing a lull, it saw a revival in the early 2000s. Bands like supergroup Kékélé brought the music back in a style reminiscent of the Buena Vista Social Club, an ensemble of musicians who wanted to play the original Cuban music.

Latin Music Rising in Pop

In the United States at the end of the twentieth century, a growing Hispanic population was driving a demand for Latin music. This environment was just right for newly minted pop star Christina Aguilera, who had scored a number of hits with her debut album in 1999.

Aguilera chose to follow up her self-titled debut with *Mi Reflejo*, an album of Spanish-language songs. The album consisted of Spanish translations of five tracks from her previous album, plus four original songs and two covers of Spanish-language songs.

Aguilera had grown up listening to Latin music in her Ecuadorian-American home and was eager to explore her heritage in music. At the time she released her Spanish language album, Aguilera did not speak the language. To make the project work, she had lyrics written out phonetically so that she could sing them convincingly. The album climbed to number one on Billboard's Top Latin Albums and Latin Pop Album charts. Aguilera also won Best Female Pop Vocal Album at the Latin Grammy Awards that year.

Aguilera was far from the only American pop artist exploring the intersections of US and Latin American sound in 1999. That same year, Puerto Rican singer Ricky Martin had released four Spanish-language albums before issuing an English-language album, *Ricky Martin*. Songs like "Livin' La Vida Loca" and "The Cup of Life" became huge hits, and the album sold more than 15 million copies.

In her 1999 debut album *On the 6*, Jennifer Lopez integrated American R&B with pop and Latin sounds. Her earlier albums each contained Spanish language tracks that acknowledged her Hispanic-American background. For her third album, *Como ama una mujer*, Lopez chose to record every song in Spanish. This album, released in 2007, would become one of the first Spanish-language albums to debut in the top 10 on the US *Billboard* charts and would garner the third-highest US sales for any Spanish-language album.

That Mexican-American Rock Sound

Pop and dance were not the only genres where Latin and American music would mix. Mexico and other areas of Latin America have long nurtured active rock and blues scenes. One of the artists who would meld American and Latin rock sounds most effectively is Carlos Santana.

Born in Jalisco, Mexico, Santana come to the United States when he was twelve years old. His family lived in San Francisco. There, he saw the rise of the counter-culture in the 1960s. He was also heavily influenced by music that included folk, blues, and jazz, as well as the guitar music played by his father, a musician in a Mexican mariachi band.

Santana's professional career began as the result of a lucky break. Famous blues harmonica player Paul Butterfield was scheduled to play a matinee show at a San Francisco music venue called the Fillmore West. When one of the original guitarists could not perform, Carlos Santana's manager suggested Santana as

The legendary Mexican guitarist Carlos Santana fuses Latin beats with rock music. During his long career, he has won ten Grammy Awards and was inducted into the Rock and Roll Hall of Fame in 1998.

a substitute. The audience was immediately won by Santana's guitar-playing, and he was soon in demand.

He soon formed the Santana Blues Band with other local musicians. The band's name was shortened to Santana when they were signed to Columbia Records. The band became noted for their unique blend of folk, jazz, blues, salsa and Afro-Cuban music.

Throughout the next two decades, Santana would continue to tap his Hispanic background when creating music. A 1983 release, *Havana Moon*, included the song "Vereda Tropical," which Santana had first heard when his father played it to serenade his mother. In 2014, Santana released *Corazón*, which included an updated version of "Oye Como Va," as well as guest appearances by a number of Latin artists. Another example of Santana's Latin influence is the 1999 hit "Smooth," recorded with Matchbox 20's Rob Thomas. The track, which features a dynamic cha-cha beat, was a huge hit.

British Reggae Artists

"As long as there's been reggae, there's been reggae in the UK, and that influence has played a massive role," British producer and DJ Ras Kwame once said to audiences on BBC Radio. Jamaica was part of the British Empire for hundreds of years, and prior to gaining independence in 1962, many Jamaicans emigrated to the United Kingdom. They brought their spirited music with them. As a result, ska and rocksteady music, and later reggae, found their way onto British radio. Soon, elements of these Caribbean music styles began to appear in the music of mainstream British artists.

In 1964, Millie Small, one of the few female ska singers to come out of Jamaica, had a surprise hit in the US and UK with her effervescent song "My Boy Lollipop." Her song is widely considered the first international ska hit, and kicked off a ska craze among British listeners and musicians. Also known in the UK as "blue beat," the music included a range of Jamaican artists who recorded in the UK, as well as English acts like The Marvels. However, ska's first wave in the UK was as brief as it was in Jamaica. As Jamaican musicians moved on to rocksteady and reggae, UK record producers moved on, as well.

At this time, reggae was gaining popularity in Jamaica and beyond. In the US, Caribbean immigrants found an African-American community that they could become a part of. However, this was largely absent in the UK. To find community, Jamaican immigrants largely embraced the growing power of reggae. As the songs found their way onto the radio, they also found fans in white British listeners and bands.

Bob Marley's influence can be heard in the many British reggae groups that emerged during the late 1970s, 1980s, and 1990s.

Like artists in other parts of the world, British music artists were inspired by increasingly prominent reggae acts. Bob Marley lived in London for a period of time, and had a heavy musical influence on bands like the Rolling Stones. Guitarist Eric Clapton would have a major hit with his cover version of Marley's "I Shot the Sheriff" in 1974. This success would help bring new American and British fans to reggae music. However, many UK reggae bands like Aswad or Steel Pulse struggled to find acceptance with black audiences. These listeners deemed them less authentic than

Jamaican-born reggae musicians. Instead, these bands found traction among a new fan-base: London punks.

Ska would also see a revival in the 1970s with the introduction of second-wave ska, a mix of punk, ska, and new wave music. Mostly released by the 2 Tone record label, second wave ska was also sometimes called "Two Tone." The goal of 2 Tone producers was to bring Britain's racially diverse population together and to ease tensions. Most of the bands on the label were ethnically diverse; as a result, audiences were, too. Important acts in 1970s and 1980s ska included Madness, The Specials, Bad Manners, The Selecter, The Beat, Akrylykz, and The Bodysnatchers.

Through a punk audience, reggae and ska found a permanent place in the UK's musical sound. The Clash covered Junior Murvin's "Police and Thieves" on their debut album. Bands like The Police and Culture Club married reggae with new wave and found audiences worldwide. UB40 would score major worldwide hits with tracks like "Red, Red Wine," which even found audiences in reggae's native Jamaica.

Today, reggae remains a staple of music in the UK, finding its way into rap, EDM and other genres, tapped by black and white artists alike. Soul II Soul singer Caron Wheeler expressed this in an interview with Britain's *Guardian* newspaper, saying, "You can't distinguish between colour any more— it's just people."

TEXT-DEPENDENT QUESTIONS

1. Who was Dizzy Gillespie's collaborator and percussionist?
2. Who originally recorded "I Shot the Sheriff"?
3. What year did Christina Aguilera release *Mi Reflejo*?

RESEARCH PROJECT

Caribbean and Latin music have made their mark all over the world. Using books from your school library along with online resources, find a contemporary artist who you enjoy who has incorporated Latin music into their sound. Learn more about which artists influenced them. Relate three to five biographical details about at least one artist.

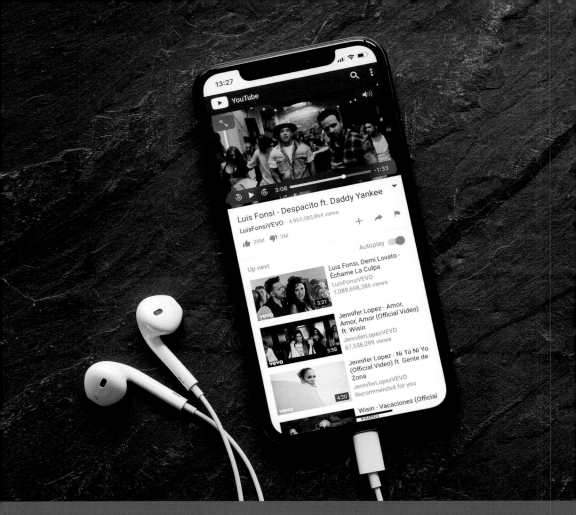

Luis Fonsi's 2017 hit "Despacito" is currently the most-viewed video in the history of YouTube, and the first video to reach 5 billion views. The hit song has drawn new attention to the Puerto Rican musical genre known as reggaetón.

 ## WORDS TO UNDERSTAND

crossover—a piece of art, typically music or film, that attains success outside of its original genre.

eponymous—being named for someone; for instance, an eponymous album.

CHAPTER 5

Latin and Caribbean Music Today

Over the past decade, the reach of Latin and Caribbean music has only gotten stronger. As recently as 2015, only three Spanish-language songs had reached the *Billboard* Hot 100. A fourth song hit the charts in 2016. That number took off the next year, however, with nineteen different Latin tracks on the *Billboard* charts. By early 2019, more than a hundred Spanish-language songs had entered the Hot 100.

There are a number of factors driving this trend. One of the most prominent is a larger number of people in the United States who speak Spanish. In 1980, only 4.9 percent of people in the United States spoke Spanish. By 2015, 11.5 percent did.

Another factor that seems to be driving the Latin music boom in the United States is the rise of music streaming services. In the past, Latin music was mostly played on Latin music radio stations. Someone listening to a top-40 or classic rock station would never hear Latin music like reggaetón. Thanks to music streaming services, the divides between music genres is becoming less rigid. Someone who is listening to a dance track by Katie Perry may see a dance track from Camila Cabello as the next suggestion. Playing a song by Demi Lovato may lead the listener to a song by Luis Fonsi. The Recording Industry Association of America's 2017 year-end report on Latin music revealed that streaming plays made up 84 percent of the profits from the Latin/Caribbean genre.

APPRECIATING TRADITIONAL CUBAN MUSIC

On a trip to Havana in 1996, the American guitarist Ry Cooder brought together a group of veteran Cuban musicians to perform traditional music, including Cuban *son*. Some of the musicians hadn't played professionally in decades, having been put out of work when the Castro government closed Havana nightclubs. But they retained impressive skills, and they recorded songs for an album. Released in 1997, *Buena Vista Social Club* earned worldwide acclaim and won a Grammy award. The ensemble toured for nearly two decades as the Orquesta Buena Vista Social Club.

Music experts also point to the popularity of dance music, which circles back, in a way, to the trends of tango, mambo, and other Latin dance music in the twentieth century. Since dance music's most prominent feature is the beats that make people move, the language of the lyrics falls in importance.

To some people, Latin music's current dominance seems to have come from out of nowhere. However, music industry experts say that it is the culmination of several years of trends. Musical trends both inside and outside the United States have led music to a moment where Latin sounds are inescapable and will continue to grow in popularity year by year.

Reggaetón Invasion

The ascendance of reggaetón is a key part of the rise of Latin music over the last several years. Today, many reggaetón acts are popular in the Caribbean and throughout the world. Artists in genres such as pop and R&B take cues from reggaetón beats. But, at the beginning, reggaetón was far from the mainstream.

Reggaetón originated in Puerto Rico in the 1990s. The music came together from influences that include hip hop, Latin American music and traditional Caribbean music. Vocals on reggaetón tracks may be rapped or sung. Beats are reminiscent of those used by Jamaican dancehall producers in the 1980s and 90s. Most reggaetón is recorded in Spanish, although many songs are either released in English or contain a combination of English and Spanish within the song. The term "reggaetón" was coined by Daddy Yankee and DJ Playero in 1994, when they used it on their album *Playero 36*.

At first, reggaetón was a form of underground music. Tracks were shared through informal markets and played at unofficial music venues. Puerto Rican youth embraced the new mix of hip hop and Latin American music and its raw, distinctly radio-unfriendly lyrics. Themes covered in early reggaetón ranged from friendship and romance to drugs, violence and poverty. The early cassettes, simply referred to as "underground" or "perreo" music, were recorded in informal studios called *marquesinas*, which were often located in public housing complexes. They were then distributed on the street instead of through more formal channels like record stores. Despite their informal nature, advances in technology meant that *marquesinas* offered independent artists high sound quality that was previously only available in professional recording studios. This high quality helped increase the popularity of early reggaetón and helped it cross socioeconomic barriers. The music became popular with kids throughout the island.

By the mid-90s, reggaetón had become popular enough that music stores were beginning to stock the music. The Puerto Rican government reacted harshly to the music's spread. In February 1995, police began a campaign against reggaetón on grounds of obscenity. Half a dozen record stores in San Juan were raided and their tapes confiscated.

Despite the controversy about reggaetón, the music continued to seep into the mainstream consciousness in Puerto Rico. Politicians began using it in election campaigns to appeal to younger voters. A rap album, *Reggae School*, was produced to help teach kids math skills. Pepsi made a commercial that featured Daddy Yankee.

Daddy Yankee was not only one of reggaetón's architects, he was instrumental in the music going global. In 2004, he released

Miami rapper Pitbull, the son of Cuban immigrants, scored a major hit in 2011 with "Give Me Everything," which was extremely popular in dance clubs. His 2016 album Dale won a Latin Billboard Award as best album.

his single "Gasolina," which experts credit with introducing Reggaetón to audiences all over the world. The song premiered within the top 10 in many markets, making this genre a global phenomenon. The song was the first reggaetón son to be nominated for Latin Grammy Record of the Year.

Reggaetón continued to make wave on charts in the United States and elsewhere. In 2007, *Wisin & Yandel: Los Extraterrestres* debuted at number 14 on the album chart, becoming the third-highest ranking reggaetón album in history. A decade later in 2017, the music video for "Despacito," by Luis Fonsi and featuring Daddy Yankee became the most viewed video in the history of YouTube. Reggaetón's place in popular music was assured.

Crossover Success

In rap and reggaetón, remixes are common. The year 2017 saw a remixed song called "Mi Gente" gain strong success. Recorded by Columbian singer J Balvin with French singer and music producer Willy William, the track is a remix of William's prior hit, "Voodoo Song."

"Mi Gente" distinguishes itself as one of a handful of songs that entered the Hot 100 charts in their Spanish language versions. While a historically rare achievement, trends suggest that this will become more common over time.

The song, in its original form, was already popular in a number of Latin American countries. It had also reached number two on the US's Hot Latin Songs chart. As a remix, it gained further traction in the United States, Argentina, Australia, Bolivia, Canada, and Costa Rica.

The video has also gained accolades for its colorful, high-action images. The video features people all over the world dancing along, as couples and in groups. The video's theme is how music, in any language, can be used to bring people together. As of January 2019, it had reached over 2.2 billion views on YouTube.

Puerto Rican rapper Wisin and singer Yandel are among the most successful reggaetón artists. Wisin Y Yandel is the only reggaetón group to win a Grammy Award, and they have won ten Billboard Latin Music Awards. They began a world tour to promote their 2018 album Los Campeones del Pueblo / "The Big Leagues."

The song was J Balvin's biggest success to date. The Columbian artist had enjoyed previous time on the charts with collaborations such as 2014's "6 AM," which featured Puerto Rican singer Farruko. That song reached number 2 on the Hot Latin Songs charts and bolstered sales of his album *La Familia*.

Latin Pop Continues Its Growth

Meanwhile, other areas of Latin music were continuing to gain audiences both within and outside of the Caribbean. Pop music has long been popular in both the United States and in Latin America. However, the two regions were far less likely to trade influences with one another until far more recently. This has changed over the past two decades, with explosive growth happening in the last few years. The move came from a handful of successful **crossover** artists who have paved the way for many more.

One of the biggest Latin pop stars today is Enrique Iglesias, who began his career in the mid-1990s under the name Enrique Martinez. When he first began recording music, he did not wish to use his real name, because he was the son of a famous Latin ballad singer, Julio Iglesias. He wanted to become successful without riding his father's coattails. He borrowed money from his childhood nanny to record a demo tape, with two songs in English and one in Spanish. Then, he brought the tape to his father's publicist, Fernan Martinez, who helped him concoct the fake name and a backstory that pitched him as a singer from Guatemala.

He was soon signed to Mexican label Fonovisa Records. Once signed, he felt it was safe to return to using his birth name. His **eponymous** debut album scored his first hit, "Si Tú Te Vas." His follow-up, *Vivir*, was released in 1997. It sold half a million copies in the first week, which was a rare accomplishment at the time for albums recorded in languages other than English. *Vivir* also saw him nominated in the Favorite Latin Artist category in the first year this genre was recognized by the American Music Awards.

A successful artist from the start, Iglesias played to sold out audiences in stadiums on his first tour. During the tour, he was supported by well-known opening acts that included Elton John, Billy Joel and Bruce Springsteen. A number of successful albums followed. However, his big crossover success was his contribution to the soundtrack for the Will Smith movie *Wild, Wild West*. The song, "Bailamos," attracted the attention of major record labels in the United States. After weeks of negotiations, he signed a multi-record deal with Interscope, a relationship that continued to generate hits and mainstream acclaim.

Recent years have seen Iglesias continuing to score hits in both English and Spanish. 2014's "Bailando" was the most-streamed song in both Spain and Mexico. In 2017, his video for "Subeme la Radio," accrued well over one billion views on YouTube.

A Puerto Rican Star Goes Mainstream

Luis Fonsi has been popular in his native Puerto Rico since the debut of his first album in 1997. However, he's only recently come to the attention of mainstream listeners outside the region with mega hit "Despacito."

His 2000 release *Eterno*, was highly successful in Latin American markets, including El Salvador, Mexico, Venezuela, and Columbia. He also was featured on Christina Aguilera's first Spanish-language album, *Mi Reflejo*. In 2002, he was featured as the opening act on Britney Spears' Dream within a Dream Tour in both Mexico and the United States. He followed up the tour with an appearance in front of billions of viewers at the 2003 Miss World pageant.

Fonsi's career continued with steady recognition within the

Enrique Inglesias, the "king of Latin pop," performs a concert in Miami.

genre of Latin music. In 2009, he won a Latin Grammy for Song of the Year for the song "Aqui Estoy Yo." By 2011, *Billboard* had designated him the "Leader of Latin Music's New Generation."

After years of steady but not explosive exposure, he scored a massive hit with "Despacito," which featured Daddy Yankee. By April 2018, the song had reached five billion views on YouTube and had become the number one hit on every Latin chart.

While he has incorporated more dance-forward EDM-inspired songs on recent albums, his music is still strongly grounded in traditional Latin sounds. 2019's *VIDA* includes a mix of English and Spanish language songs, including "Echame la Culpa," a bilingual hit recorded with Demi Lovato. He pays tribute to the Caribbean region elsewhere on the album with tracks like "Calypso."

The crossover appeal of an artist like Fonsi continues to show the progression of Latin sounds from niche interest to lasting and growing mainstream appeal.

Scan here to see Luis Fonsi and Demi Lovato collaborate on "Échame La Culpa":

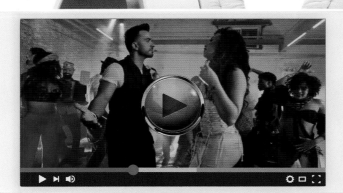

Barbadian singer Rihanna has won nine Grammy Awards and thirteen American Music Awards. Her influence goes far beyond music, though; she has helped to build schools and hospitals in Barbados, and in 2017 she was named Harvard University's "Humanitarian of the Year."

Barbadian Pop Star Rules the World

Hit-making producer Evan Rogers was visiting family in Barbados when he encountered a teenage singer named Rihanna. She was performing with a girl group she'd formed at her high school. Soon, she and Rogers had produced a demo, which she used to audition for hip-hop star and entertainment mogul Jay Z. The demo yielded her a six-album deal with Def Jam. Rihanna left Barbados immediately to relocate to Los Angeles and begin her recording career.

Growing up in Barbados, Rihanna did not have exposure to a lot of music from outside the islands. Mostly, she listened to local music like soca, reggae, and hip-hop. Caribbean rhythm and sound is deeply apparent in Rihanna's first two albums, especially in songs like "Pon de Replay." She has also covered songs by her favorite musician, Bob Marley, and keeps a shrine to Marley in her home.

Like other artists from the Caribbean region, Rihanna continues to inspire. Artists like Lorde, Selena Gomez, Justin Bieber, Demi Lovato, and Grimes all cite her as an influence. Both the British boy band The Wanted and Nigerian pop star Orezi have named songs for her.

Camila Cabello's Cuban Influence

Cuban-American singer Camila Cabello first rose to prominence as part of the girl group Fifth Harmony. While Fifth Harmony's focus was on mainstream pop and R&B, Camila began immediately distinguishing herself as a solo artist with her mix of R&B and music influenced by her Cuban heritage.

While Cabello was born in Cuba, her father was originally from Mexico. Cabello spent her early life traveling back and forth between Havana and Mexico City before her family resettled in the US in Miami.

She auditioned for *The X Factor* in 2012 with a performance of Aretha Franklin's seminal hit "Respect." However, because the

Since leaving Fifth Harmony in 2016, Cuban-American singer Camila Cabello has scored several solo hits, including the #1 smash "Havana" in 2017.

show was unable to secure rights to the song, her audition was not featured in the series. Despite being eliminated early in the show, she was brought back later on as part of the ensemble that later became Fifth Harmony.

Her tenure with the girl group did not last long. By 2016, she had departed from the group and begun collaborating with artists like Machine Gun Kelly and Shawn Mendez. A collaboration with Pitbull and J Balvin, "Hey Ma," was recorded for the soundtrack of *The Fate of the Furious* (2017). The Spanish language single was soon followed by a popular English language one.

When her debut studio album *Camila* was released in 2018, it premiered at #1 on the *Billboard* album chart. The salsa-inspired lead single "Havana" topped the charts in the United States, the UK, and several other countries. The song's video continues to play up the Latin flavor, with references to the Latin soap operas known as *telenovelas* and a movie within the video that evokes the Latin dance clubs of the 1950s.

Far from being a song with niche appeal, the song and video were instant mainstream successes. The video received four nominations at the 2018 MTV Video Music Awards: Video of the Year (which it won), Song of the Year, Best Choreography, and Best Pop Video.

Latin Flavor in Rap

Along with pop and reggaetón, more standard hip hop music has continued to be a source of success for Latin and Latin-American artists. Some of the top artists of today emigrated to the United States from the Caribbean or were born in the states to Caribbean or Latin American parents.

Nicki Minaj emigrated from her native Trinidad and Tobago to the Queens borough of New York City when she was just five years old. However, she is still deeply committed to the place where she was born. Tropical beats support her 2015 Top-100 hit "Trini Dem Girls." In 2018, she raised funds for the people of Trinidad to help them cope with the after effects of deadly flooding.

Nowhere is the rising influence of social media on mainstream music more apparent than in the career of Caribbean-American rap star Cardi B. Born in New York to a Trinidadian mother and a Dominican father, Cardi B first rose to prominence after a number of her videos went viral on Instagram and Vine. She soon joined the cast of the VH1 reality series *Love & Hip Hop: New York* for its sixth season, and became a breakout star. She left after two seasons to pursue her career in music.

A native of Trinidad and Tobago, Nicki Minaj has become one of the most influential female rappers of all time.

Cardi B performs at the 2017 MTV Video Music Awards. Her music draws on her strong Caribbean roots.

Cardi B's musical debut began with an appearance on Jamaican reggae fusion artist Shaggy's remix of his song "Boom Boom." Appearances on compilations and guest vocals on other artists' tracks soon followed. She signed with a major record label in 2017 and was soon nominated for two awards at the 2017 BET Awards: Best Female Hip-Hop Artist and Best New Artist.

In 2018, she collaborated with DJ Snake on the song "Taki Taki," which entered the top 20 on the *Billboard* Hot 100 at its debut. The song garnered more than a billion views on YouTube and a strong following among audiences in Hispanic countries. *People en Español* magazine named Cardi B the "Star of the Year."

While Cardi B is native to the United States, Caribbean music has always been a strong influence. She cites the work of Puerto Rican rapper Ivy Queen and Jamaican dancehall artist Spice as inspirations, along with American rapper Missy Elliot.

The Blending of Sounds Continues

Throughout the story of the Caribbean and Latin America, cultural and musical influences have met, blended and created something new. With the new reach of streaming and social media, this trend will only continue to grow stronger and more prevalent. While many of these changes are unprecedented, a historical path can be seen. Recording company professionals looking for the next big act are looking outside the United States to Venezuela, Columbia and beyond. Music from other regions and genres continues to season the nourishing stew of Caribbean music, which Caribbean music continues to feed creativity to the rest of the world.

TEXT-DEPENDENT QUESTIONS

1. What are three factors that have driven the rise of Latin and Caribbean music in the US?

2. Where was Nicki Minaj born?

3. What year was Enrique Iglesias first nominated for a Favorite Latin Artist award at the American Music Awards?

RESEARCH PROJECT

Puerto Rico is a Commonwealth of the United States. Using your school library and trusted internet sources, research Puerto Rico's history. What is a commonwealth and how does it differ from a state? Who are some famous musical artists to come from Puerto Rico? What impact have they had on music and culture in the US?

CHAPTER NOTES

p. 16: "two wings of the same bird," Lola Rodríguez de Tió, "A Cuba," in *Mi Libro de Cuba: Poesías* (Havana, Cuba: Imprenta La Moderna, 1893), p. 6.

p. 25: "The transition from being an African …" Peter Manuel, *Caribbean Currents: Caribbean Music from Rumba to Reggae* (Philadelphia: Temple University Press, 2006)

p. 39: "The music, dance and poetry …" United Nations Educational, Scientific, and Cultural Organization, "Tango," (2009). https://ich.unesco.org/en/RL/tango-00258

p. 45: "In my opinion, the true salsa sound … " Sergio George, quoted in Manuel, *Caribbean Currents: Caribbean Music from Rumba to Reggae*, p. 91.

p. 54: "similar to a nuclear weapon," Dizzy Gillespie, quoted in Keith Murphy, "The Night Latin Jazz Was Born," OZY (February 19, 2018). https://www.ozy. com/flashback/the-night-latin-jazz-was-born/83437

p. 54: "they'd never seen a marriage …" Dizzy Gillespie, quoted in Murphy, "The Night Latin Jazz Was Born."

p. 57: "What else have I got to sell …" Tito Puente, quoted in "On This Day: The Mambo King Is Born," The History Channel (December 13, 2018). https://www.history.com/this-day-in-history/mambo-king-tito-puente-is-born

p. 64: "As long as there's been reggae …" DJ Ras , quoted in Baz Dreisinger, "Reggae in the UK: A Steady Force," National Public Radio (March 21, 2012). https://www.npr.org/sections/therecord/2012/03/21/149062967/reggae-in-the-u-k-a-steady-force

p. 66: "You can't distinguish between colour any more—it's just people," Caron Wheeler, quoted in "Reggae: the Sound that Revolutionised Britain," *The Guardian* (January 29, 2011). https://www.theguardian.com/music/2011/jan/30/reggae-revolutionary-bob-marley-britain

A&R department—the talent department at a record label, which is responsible for finding artists and acquiring songs for them to record. A&R stands for "artists and repertoire."

audio mixing—the process by which multiple sounds are combined into a finished song. The music producer often uses a mixing console to manipulate or enhance each source sound's volume and dynamics.

ballad—a folk song that narrates a story in short stanzas.

beat—the steady pulse that listeners feel in a musical piece.

bootleg—an unauthorized recording of a song.

chord—three or more tones played at the same time.

copyright—the exclusive legal right to control the publication or reproduction of artistic works, such as songs, books, or movies. Musicians protect their original songs through copyright to prevent other people from stealing their songs, lyrics, or musical tunes. The period of copyright protection is generally seventy years after the death of the creator of the work.

demo—short for "demonstration recording," a song that that is professionally produced and recorded to demonstrate the ability of a musician or musical group.

harmony—the simultaneous combination of tones or pitches, especially when blended into chords that are pleasing to the ear.

hook—the "catchy" part of a song that makes people want to hear it repeatedly. The hook can be lyrical or musical. It is often the title of the song, and is usually repeated frequently throughout the song.

hymn—a song of religious worship.

instrumentation—the way a song's composer or arranger assigns elements of the music to specific instruments. When done for an orchestra, this is called "orchestration."

lyrics—the words of a song.

mastering—the final process of preparing a mixed recording for commercial distribution.

measure—a way of organizing music according to its rhythmic structure. Each measure, or "bar," includes a certain number of beats.

pitch—term used to describe how high or low a note sounds. Pitch is determined by the note's frequency, or the number of complete oscillations per second of energy as sound in the form of sound-waves.

producer—the person in charge of making a record. Chooses the musicians, instrumentation, and songs for the project, and oversees it to completion, often in collaboration with the recording artist and staff of the record company.

riff—a short repeated phrase in popular music and jazz, typically used as an introduction or refrain in a song.

rhythm—a strong, regular, repeated pattern of musical sounds.

scale—a sequence of notes in either descending or ascending order.

signature song—a song that a popular music artist or band is most known for or associated with, usually one of their biggest hits. The most popular artists can have more than one signature song.

solo—a piece of music, or a passage in a piece of music, that is performed by one musician.

tempo—the speed at which a piece of music is played.

1492: Christopher Columbus first arrives in the Caribbean and encounters the Taino people. While the area's indigenous people did not survive encounters with European settlers, their instruments and some religious practices persisted.

1502: Nicolás de Ovando brings 2,500 Spanish settlers to the island of Hispanola. This is the first full European settlement in the area and the beginning of the colonial influence on Caribbean music.

1518: A shipment of 4,000 enslaved people are brought to Jamaica. They would be sold to plantation owners throughout the region and come to live on islands throughout the Caribbean.

1762: English forces briefly take possession of Cuba. They introduce contredanse, which will live on as *danzón*, Cuba's national dance.

1800s: The tango is created in Uruguay and Argentina.

1921: Rudolph Valentino launches the tango craze by performing the dance in the silent movie *The Four Horsemen of the Apocalypse*.

1922: The first commercial radio station in Cuba goes on the air.

1947: Dizzy Gillespie performs Latin Jazz at Carnegie Hall.

1950s: The Bolivian government forms a commission to encourage the appreciation of indigenous music. A Bolivian folk revival results.

1958: Ritchie Valens releases "La Bamba."

1959: Fidel Castro takes control of Cuba. The ensuing embargo ends the flow of Cuban music and musicians to the United States.

1962: Tito Puente records "Oye Como Va."

1968: The first reggae record, "Bangarang," is released.

1973: "Salsa" is first used on television to describe a genre of music. The Jamaican crime film *The Harder They Come* and its soundtrack help to launch reggae into the American consciousness.

1974: Eric Clapton's cover of Bob Marley's "I Shot the Sheriff" becomes his first #1 hit.

1987: "La Bamba" returns to the charts when Los Lobos releases a version to accompany a biopic about Ritchie Valens.

1999: Carlos Santana records "Smooth" with Rob Thomas.

2000: Christina Aguilera releases her first Spanish-language album, *Mi Reflejo*.

2002: Tito Puente's *Dance Mania* is added to the National Recording Registry.

2004: "Gasolina" by Daddy Yankee debuts on the top 10 in music markets around the world.

2007: Jennifer Lopez releases *Como ama una mujer*, which garners the third-highest US sales for any Spanish-language album.

2009: The tango is added to the UNESCO Intangible Cultural Heritage List after a joint proposal from Uruguay and Argentina.

2014: "6 AM" is released by Columbian artist J Balvin in collaboration with Puerto Rican singer Farruko.

2017: "Despacito" is released and becomes a major hit.

Manuel, Peter. *Caribbean Currents: Caribbean Music from Rumba to Reggae.* Philadelphia: Temple University Press, 2006.

Roberts, John Storm *The Latin Tinge: The Impact of Latin American Music on the United States*. New York: Oxford University Press, 1979.

Kurlanksy, Mark. *Havana: A Subtropical Delirium*. New York: Bloomsbury USA, 2017.

Bergman, Billy *Hot Sauces: Latin and Caribbean Pop*. New York: Quill, 1985.

Thompson, Dave *Reggae & Caribbean Music: The Essential Listening Companion*. San Francisco: Backbeat Books, 2002.

Ziff, John. *Cuban Music, Dance, and Celebrations*. Philadelphia: Mason Crest, 2018.

https://www.rollingstone.com/music/music-latin/
The Latin Music category of *Rolling Stone* magazine contains news and reviews related to Latin music, both in the United States and abroad.

https://www.billboard.com/latin
Billboard magazine's Latin category charts the popularity of Latin songs and albums. The section also contains news and reviews of Latin and Caribbean music.

https://www.youtube.com/channel/UC_qo8SpCCQ8m5zxoJDaqPbw
YouTube's Latin Pop topic showcases music from or influenced by Latin America.

https://open.spotify.com/genre/latin-page
Spotify's Latin music page is a parent page that provides access to a wide range of Latin music. From the top level page, curious listeners can access sub channels that include reggaetón, Latin pop, regional Mexican music, and more.

http://www.pbs.org/buenavista/
From PBS, this companion website to the documentary film *Buena Vista Social Club* offers a timeline of Cuba's musical history, brief essays, interviews, photographs, and more.

INDEX

AUTHOR'S BIOGRAPHY

LARA STEWART MANETTA is a writer and full-time liveaboard sailor. She studied journalism at the University of South Florida and first began writing professionally about music in the early 2000s. She became entranced with the music of Latin America and the Caribbean while planning a sailing trip to the area. Her previous work includes music reviews, interviews with artists and promotional work.

CREDITS